12 Step Prayers
for A Way Out

12 Step Prayers *f o r* A Way Out

by Friends in Recovery
with Jerry S.

Prayers compiled and written
by Bill Pittman

RPI PUBLISHING, INC.   SAN DIEGO

Published by
RPI Publishing, Inc.
1201 Knoxville Street
San Diego, CA 92110-3718
(619) 275-1350

Library of Congress Cataloging-in-Publication Data
12 step prayers for a way out / by Friends in Recovery with
Jerry S. ; prayers compiled and written by Bill Pittman.
p.   cm.
ISBN 0-941405-29-X (pbk.)
1. Recovering addicts—Prayer-books and devotions—English.
2. Recovering addicts—Religious life. I. Jerry S. II. Pittman,
Bill, 1947– . III. Friends in Recovery. IV. Title: Twelve step
prayers for a way out.
BL624.5.A135   1993
242′.4—dc20   93-11016
                                                                      CIP

Printed in the United States of America
10 9 8 7 6 5 4 3 2 1

Contents

*T*he Twelve Steps

1. We admitted we were powerless over the effects of addiction — that our lives had become unmanageable.
2. Came to believe that a Power greater than ourselves could restore us to wholeness.
3. Made a decision to turn our will and our lives over to the care of God *as we understood God*.
4. Made a searching and fearless moral inventory of ourselves.
5. Admitted to God, to ourselves, and to another human being the exact nature of our wrongs.
6. Were entirely ready to work in partnership with God to remove our ineffective behavior.
7. Humbly asked God to help us remove our shortcomings.
8. Made a list of all persons we had harmed and became willing to make amends to them all.
9. Made direct amends to such people wherever possible, except when to do so would injure them or others.
10. Continued to take personal inventory and, when we were wrong, promptly admitted it.
11. Sought through prayer and meditation to improve our conscious contact with God *as we understood God*, praying only for knowledge of God's will for us and for the power to carry that out.
12. Having had a spiritual awakening as the result of these steps, we tried to carry this message to others, and to practice these principles in all our affairs.

The Twelve Steps of Alcoholics Anonymous

1. We admitted we were powerless over alcohol—that our lives had become unmanageable.
2. Came to believe that a Power greater than ourselves could restore us to sanity.
3. Made a decision to turn our will and our lives over to the care of God *as we understood Him.*
4. Made a searching and fearless moral inventory of ourselves.
5. Admitted to God, to ourselves, and to another human being the exact nature of our wrongs.
6. Were entirely ready to have God remove all these defects of character.
7. Humbly asked Him to remove our shortcomings.
8. Made a list of all persons we had harmed, and became willing to make amends to them all.
9. Made direct amends to such people wherever possible, except when to do so would injure them or others.
10. Continued to take personal inventory and when we were wrong promptly admitted it.
11. Sought through prayer and meditation to improve our conscious contact with God, *as we understood Him,* praying only for knowledge of His will for us and the power to carry that out.
12. Having had a spiritual awakening as the result of these steps, we tried to carry this message to alcoholics, and to practice these principles in all our affairs.

*I*ntroduction

❧ THE WOMAN SAT CONDEMNED BY JUDGE AND JURY. She had committed many cruel and serious offenses since her adolescence. Now she faced imprisonment for the rest of her life. But before the judge pronounced his sentence, he sincerely asked, "What caused you to become the woman you are?"

She answered, "When I was a little girl, I lived alone with my mother. Mom had to work two jobs to keep a roof over my head and food in my mouth. At dusk, the other kids were called away from the streets by the familiar voices of their parents. Someone would cry out, 'Mary, it's time for supper!' or 'Billy, come in now—it's getting dark!' But nobody ever called out my name. My mom was at work when others were eating supper. I sat alone in the kitchen, and I choked on the cold food from the icebox. I was always asleep when Mom came home. Oh, how I wished that someone would call out for me! Maybe I'd be different, Your Honor, if someone had called out my name."

It may not be hard for many of us in recovery to imagine growing up alone. Maybe we really didn't speak to our parents. And when our parents spoke to us, it was often to shout and condemn. The problem is that, with little or no proper parental direction, many of us grew up not knowing how to live. The only type of communication that many of us know is abusive and loud or silent and brooding, never genuine and sincere. We may not have learned about relationships, responsibility, cooperation, and commitment. Or we may be socially crippled, all because we never really communicated with our parents or guardians.

We cannot carry these broken social and faulty communication patterns into our recovery. We need to talk to our Higher Power, and to listen for the answer. God alone can effectively direct our lives. Our Higher Power's will and plan for us is best. So we must learn to pray—to communicate with God, and learn to listen—to meditate.

Step Eleven says, "Sought through prayer and meditation to improve our conscious contact with God as we understood God, praying only for knowledge of God's will for us and for the power to carry that out." We have seen the wisdom and effectiveness of the Twelve-Step program, but we sometimes balk when we come to the actions prescribed in this eleventh step—especially prayer. We may question the usefulness of prayer, or we may passively ignore the practice of it by not consciously reaching out to our Higher Power on a daily basis.

Most resistance to prayer doesn't come from a disbelief in God. We have accepted Step Two, and with it, we have come to believe in a power greater than ourselves. Our resistance to prayer stems from the simple fact that many of us were never really taught how to pray. But if we are to succeed in our Twelve-Step program, we will succeed only to the degree that we are willing to reach out to our Higher Power.

The Twelve-Step program is not a human-powered program. God is the source of our power and our progress. Therefore, daily contact with our Higher Power is all-important. Remember that the Twelve-Step program is spiritual. God becomes known to us through the Twelve Steps without any religious effort on our part. Contact with our Higher Power, whether we articulate it in prayer or sit, silent and attentive, in meditation, is our vital link to recovery.

This book is foremost a guide to Twelve-Step oriented prayer. It includes a resource of prayers that have been specifically written and collected for Twelve-Step program use and application. This text works as a companion and aid for the effective use of *The 12 Steps —A Way Out* (Recovery Publications, Inc., 1987).

PRAYER AND THE TWELVE-STEP PROGRAM

Twelve-Step prayers differ from other prayers. In Twelve-Step programs we come to understand that prayer isn't a self-indulgent plea for favors. We learn that our Higher Power cannot be manipulated by our pleading. We replace demanding prayers and wish lists with prayers that clearly ask for knowledge of God's will.

In the Twelve-Step program we are encouraged to pray, to maintain contact with our Higher Power. As participants in the program, we strive to season our lives and our recovery with continual prayer. We covet our Higher Power's participation in our recovery. We use prayer as a daily invitation to God to stay involved in our lives, and to help us in our journey.

PRAYER AND GOD'S WILL

In this program it is important that we develop a comforting relationship with our Higher Power. God as we understand God in this program is forgiving, tolerant, and understanding of our weaknesses and mistakes. Our Higher Power is not to be feared or avoided. We will not be retaliated against or belittled because of our frailties or blemishes. The Higher Power we come to know through this program is a God we can trust.

Once we trust our Higher Power, we begin to see that our very best prayer is a request to know God's will for our lives. Turning our lives over to our Higher Power, admitting that we are powerless to control them as they are, means that we understand that God does indeed have a better idea. When we pray this way, we come to see perhaps the most evident wisdom of the Twelve Steps, that we cannot and do not have to control our lives.

More than fifty years ago, the authors of the Twelve Steps pointed out, in the Big Book of Alcoholics Anonymous, that our problems are not rooted in one particular compulsion, addiction, or drug of choice. They are rooted in the issue of who is in control of our lives. By the time we grasp the direction and aim of the Twelve Steps, we understand that our Higher Power is in control because we have surrendered our lives to God's care. That surrender becomes our greatest source of serenity.

Step One helps us admit our powerlessness. Step Two opens our eyes to a power greater than ourselves. Step Three brings us to a place of decision as we turn our will and lives over to our Higher Power. And Steps Four through Ten help us to see our failures and defects and to humbly seek God's help in our continual healing. In working the first ten steps, we learn to rely upon our Higher Power as a source of encouragement and support. Learning new ways of communicating with our Higher Power can only enhance our recovery.

Our best and sanest prayer is, "Thy will be done." God's will is still best. Our will and our control only brought us sorrow, pain, and mismanagement. Our Higher Power's will brings peace and order into our lives.

THE PRACTICE
OF PRAYER

We in recovery want to develop a lifestyle of regular prayer and communication with our Higher Power, not just a few minutes wedged into the day. Although it seems absurd, it is possible to "pray without ceasing." Prayer, rightly understood, is a way of life that provides peace and serenity in our daily activities.

Many of us bristle when prayer disciplines and regimens are thrust in our faces. The idea of regimen, discipline, rules, and directives can rub us the wrong way. We've learned to live by maxims such as "Easy Does It," "Let Go and Let God" and "Go with the Flow." For us, prayer needs to be a free flow of communication to a person—the person of our Higher Power. And like communication with any person, prayer must be multidimensional and dynamic, a living connection.

Brother Lawrence, a seventeenth-century monk who served his monastery as cook, coined the phrase "practicing the presence of God." That is exactly the goal of Twelve-Step prayer: to improve and maintain our conscious contact with our Higher Power, to practice our Higher Power's presence continually.

The practice of God's presence for the purpose of prayer is best learned through meditation. In meditation we learn how to silence our own internal activities, thoughts, and anxieties, and to center on our Higher Power's presence in our lives and in the world around us. Although meditation is a separate subject, it is, nevertheless, the very foundation on which real prayer is built.

Understanding or knowing about the continual practice of prayer is one thing. Doing it is another. We are creatures of habit, and we need established and set-aside times and places of prayer. We need to take time for talking to our Higher Power, regardless of how long it takes. With that in mind, let us search our hearts, our daily routines, and our homes for a time and place of daily prayer. The daily appointments we make and keep with our Higher Power will encourage the lifestyle of prayer that we seek.

THE FOLLOWING PRAYERS ARE INTENDED TO HELP US express to our Higher Power the unique life we live in the Twelve-Step program. The prayers are organized according to the individual steps.

Each person reading this book will be at his or her own place in working the Twelve Steps. However, once we've been with the program for a while, we come to see that we don't just work the steps once and then never pay attention to them again. For instance, a person who has worked through the steps and gotten into recovery from a drinking problem may go back and work through the steps with regard to relationship problems. Say that person is at Step Four. But, around issues of her sobriety, she may want to use some of the prayers from the later steps. Or, on a particularly bad day, she may want to go back and pray prayers relating to Step Two, prayers that will remind her that there really is a Higher Power who can restore her to wholeness.

If you are new to the Twelve-Step recovery program, I invite you to read this book from beginning to end and to use the prayers to form the basis of your daily prayer habit. If you're an old hand, I also invite you to read through the book from beginning to end, and then to go to those steps with which you are working, on any given day, to find the prayers that may help you articulate your conversation with God.

These prayers acknowledge and yield to the supremacy of God's will. They also foster conversation and intimacy with our Higher Power. We can use them as tools in our daily communications with God and as examples or models as we develop our own personal expressions of prayer to our Higher Power.

1

Prayers *f o r* Step One

We admitted we were powerless over the effects of addiction — that our lives had become unmanageable.

❦ "WHAT'S WRONG WITH GRAMPS, MOMMY?"

"Nothing, dear, he'll be fine. Let's be still so Grams can talk on the phone." But seven-year-old Brooke wasn't so sure. Gramps looked awful and gray there on the sofa. Brooke strained to hear Grams talking to the doctor.

"Well, doctor," Grams tried to speak lowly, but the low button on her voice didn't work very well anymore. "He says he can't breathe..."

"Hang up the damn phone," Gramps barked. "I don't want no kid doctor knowing my business. You tell him to have Doc Johnson call me."

"Dear, Doctor Johnson retired last year."

"Well then maybe it's time I retire, too—for good." Gramps looked bad, but Brooke moved near him and reached out for his callused and powerful hand, which now hung down from the narrow sofa.

"Gramps, are you gonna die?"

"Brooke, don't ask your grandpa that. That's silly. Of course he's not going to die." As Brooke's mom spoke, she pulled her daughter back and broke her timid grasp on Gramps's hand.

"I'll die when I'm damn good and ready. And I ain't ready..."

"Daddy! Daddy!" Brooke's mom cried as Gramps's eyes rolled upward. "Mom! Something's wrong, call 9-1-1. He's not..."

Brooke ran to the corner. She watched her grandma and mother explode in concern around Gramps, as he lay still.

Every move, every word, every tear was forever etched in the little girl's memory. She stood frozen, recording it all. Her gruff and stern grandfather's boast was now silent. The power of his words and life now quiet. The grasp of his mighty hands now released. The height of his noble stature now fallen.

He was always in control, in charge, but Brooke watched as others took control. A paramedic pulled him to the floor and blew air into lungs that could no longer accept or expel it. Another pushed on a heart that never awoke.

GRAMPS WAS A POWERFUL MAN. HE TOOK CHARGE OF every detail of life, but he was powerless in the face of death. Control and manageability are illusions. His words were an empty boast. As Emily Dickinson said, "Because I could not stop for death / He kindly stopped for me."

The truth is we are never really in control. For every one thing we manage to juggle in our grasp, a hundred other things slip through our hands. The sooner we admit to our powerlessness and need, the better.

Step One is just what it sounds like — our first significant step toward recovery. And that important step begins with an admission of defeat. It doesn't matter who we admit it to, but it matters that we admit that we are powerless over the effects of our addiction or compulsion. Even more, we admit that our lives are unmanageable the way they are. When we make this admission and really mean it, life begins again. Gramps can't come back, but we can. With the help of the Twelve Steps we can find a way out of the painful mess we have called life.

In Step One we learn through the pain and unmanage-ability of our lives that we cannot control our own lives or the lives of others. Under our own management, our lives have failed, not prospered. In Step One, all we need do is admit this. Therefore, the prayer in Step One is a cry of admission and surrender. But more, it is a complaint, a plea for help from someone caught in an unmanageable condition.

In Step One we might cry out, "That's it! I quit! I can't manage life on my own. Life stinks, and I don't know how to change." This "prayer" may or may not be directed to our Higher Power. It may not even feel like a prayer. However, it is the beginning of surrender that is necessary for coming to believe in a Higher Power. It is an honest cry of pain and a genuine call for help.

First Step Prayer

Today, I ask for help with my addiction. Denial has kept me from seeing how powerless I am and how my life is unmanageable. I need to learn and remember that I have an incurable illness and that abstinence is the only way to deal with it.

To Be Honest, God

To be honest, I'm not sure who I'm praying to.
Maybe I'm talking to myself, but...

To be honest, I can't take anymore.
My life is a failure, I feel like a...

To be honest, I want to die, I want to quit,
I want to quit hurting me, I want to quit hurting them.

To be honest, I don't know what to do.
For the first time, I'm really lost...

To be honest, I don't know if anyone hears me,
But if someone hears, please come find me.

Reliance on God

O Higher Power,
never let me think
that I can stand by myself,
and not need you.

Sailor's Prayer

Dear God, be good to me. The sea is so wide, and my
boat is so small.

Let Go, Let God

Higher Power, help me to understand:

To "let go" does not mean to stop caring; it means I can't
   do it for someone else.
To "let go" is not to enable but to allow learning from
   natural consequences.
To "let go" is to admit powerlessness, which means the
   outcome is not in my hands.

To "let go" is not to try to change or blame another; it's
    to make the most of myself.

To "let go" is not to care for but to care about.

To "let go" is not to fix but to be supportive.

To "let go" is not to judge but to allow another to be a
    human being.

To "let go" is not to protect; it's to permit another to face
    reality.

To "let go" is not to deny but to accept.

To "let go" is not to nag, scold, or argue but instead to
    search out my own shortcomings and correct them.

To "let go" is not to adjust everything to my desires but
    to take each day as it comes and cherish myself in it.

2

Prayers *f o r* Step Two

Came to believe that a Power greater than ourselves could restore us to wholeness.

❦ SCOTT IS TWENTY-THREE, BUT HE HAS ALREADY
lived a lifetime. In fact, some of his friends have already
finished with life, but not by choice. Scott's father, who is
just a vague memory, is very successful and lives far away.
He visited once when Scott was sixteen. He bought Scott a
car, after Scott's mom approved. She didn't approve at first.
But when Scott yielded to her manipulation, jumped
through her hoops, and played her games, she finally
agreed. Scott's father sends him money, but it still goes
through Scott's mom who controls every penny. So he cons
her for every dime his dad sends, only to use it to try to kill
his pain and anger.

Some time ago, Scott's mom got religion. She just knows
that her dogmatic church will change Scott, help him kick
drugs, get new friends, and find meaning in his life. So now
Scott gets his allowance only if he goes to church with her.
Scott is easy to notice in his mother's strict church. He gets
up several times during the service, squirms when he is
seated, and bolts out the door during the final prayer. As
the harsh preacher screams out condemnation against por-
nography, drunkenness, drugs, lust, or sin, Scott fumes
because he knows that he is guilty as charged. Just below
Scott's anger lies his shame; and just below his shame, lies
his despair.

As he waits alone in the parking lot, he is anything but
uplifted or encouraged. He hates these people and their
God. No amount of preaching or condemnation will bring

him to the point in his life where he is ready to make changes and improve the quality of his life.

Condemnation and judgment has no power to change us. In fact, the condemnation and judgment of others tends to ground us in our self-defeating behavior. What changes us is love, unconditional love. Our Higher Power offers this kind of love for us.

The idea of a loving Higher Power may seem very hard to believe or accept at first. So in the beginning we can look for our Higher Power's love and acceptance from our program members. In the program we will find love, not judgment. When we are being judged, we squirm. But when we are being loved, we change.

Many of us who are in recovery have, at one time or another, felt uncomfortable in church. Religion might have been shoved down our throats, leaving us choking for spiritual sustenance. Religion might have been offered as a bribe, like it is to Scott. We may have been harshly judged and never really loved. We may have a very distorted view of God. We may see God like the harsh preacher, the condemning church, the faraway father, the meddling mother, or others. But our recovery depends upon knowing this simple truth: Our Higher Power is good, and unconditionally loves us.

The heart of Tradition Two, which is read in Twelve-Step meetings, reminds us that "there is but one ultimate authority—a loving God." The program teaches us that our Higher Power, however we may understand that power, provides the love, power, and direction we need to guide us in our recovery.

If you're angry at God, that's OK; just remember that the God you're angry at is not the God of this program.

———————

AS WE STAND IN THE DOORWAY LEADING TO THE second step, we may feel rather empty and wanting because of Step One. But that's OK—this is exactly where we belong in the beginning. In Step Two, we begin to exercise faith—faith that our Higher Power provides. We simply come to believe that a power greater than ourselves can restore us to wholeness (and take care of us). We needn't even put a name on our Higher Power in Step Two. We simply exercise the bud of faith that is beginning to grow in our hearts.

A Step Two prayer is an implied prayer of trust. We might pray, "Higher Power, somehow I know that you can hear me—don't ask me how. I also know that you can help me find my way back to wholeness."

Second Step Prayer

I pray for an open mind so I may come to believe in a power greater than myself. I pray for humility and the continued opportunity to increase my faith. I don't want to be crazy anymore.

Greater Than Myself

Higher Power,
The sky over my head,
The generations that came before,
The stars that shine above,
The world and its creatures,

The body in which I live,
The sun that warms,
The air I breathe,
The order and way of the universe,
All these things are greater than I am.
Who am I to doubt you God?

A Beginner's Prayer

Lord, I want to love you, yet I am not sure.
I want to trust you, yet I am afraid of being taken in.
I know I need you, but I am ashamed of the need.
I want to pray, but I am afraid of being a hypocrite.
I need my independence, yet I fear to be alone.
I want to belong, yet I must be myself.
Take me, Lord, yet leave me alone.
Lord, I believe; help thou my unbelief.
O Lord, if you are there,
you do understand, don't you?
Give me what I need,
but leave me free to choose.
Help me work it out my own way,
but don't let me go.
Let me understand myself,
but don't let me despair.
Come unto me, O Lord,
I want you there.
Lighten my darkness,
but don't dazzle me.
Help me to see what I need to do,
and give me strength to do it.
O Lord, I believe;
help thou my unbelief.

Against Temptations

May the strength of my Higher Power guide me.
May the power of God preserve me.
May the wisdom of my Higher Power instruct me.
May the hand of God protect me.
May the way of God direct me.
May the shield of God defend me.
And may the presence of, and belief in, my Higher Power
    guard me against the temptations of the world.

Lord, I'm Hurting

Yes, Lord, I hurt.
The pain is deep,
And I feel the mountains
Are so steep.
I cannot seem to stand.
Please, dear Lord,
Take my hand.
I cannot seem
To find my way.
For me the sun
Is not shining today.
I know you're there;
I've felt your presence near
But now, my Lord,
My heart is gripped with fear.
Lord, help the sun to shine
And to know
That you are mine.
Heal this pain I feel;
Make your presence

Very real.
Today, Lord, I give you all.
Help me, dear Lord,
Not to fall.
And if I fall,
Hold me tight,
So I can feel
Your strength and might.

Self-Respect Prayer

O God, teach me that self-respect cannot be hunted. It cannot be purchased. It is never for sale. It comes to me when I am alone, in quiet moments, in quiet places, when I suddenly realize that, knowing the *good*, I have done it; knowing the *beautiful*, I have served it; knowing the *truth*, I have spoken it.

Prayer for the Hurried

Lord, slow me down.

Ease the pounding of my heart by quieting my mind. Steady my hurried pace. Give me, in the confusion of my day, the calmness of the everlasting hills. Break the tension of my nerves and muscles. Help me to know the magical, restoring power of sleep.

Teach me to take minute vacations by slowing down to look at a flower, a cloud, to chat with a friend, to pat a dog, to read a few lines from a good book. Remind me that the race is not always to the swift, that there is more to life than increasing speed.

Let me look upward into the branches of the towering oak and know that it grew great and strong because it grew slowly and well.

Lord, slow me down. Inspire me to send my roots deep into the soil of life's enduring values that I may grow toward the stars of my great destiny.

Make Me

God, who touches earth with beauty,
Make me lovely, too;
With your spirit re-create me,
Make my heart anew.

Like your springs and running waters,
Make me crystal pure;
Like your rocks of towering grandeur
Make me strong and sure.

Like your dancing waves in sunlight,
Make me glad and free;
Like the straightness of the pine trees
Let me upright be.

Like the arching of the heavens,
Lift my thoughts above;
Turn my dreams to noble action,
Ministries of love.

God, who touches earth with beauty,
Make me lovely, too;
Keep me ever, by your spirit,
Pure and strong and true.

3

Prayers
f o r
Step Three

---

*Made a decision to turn our will
and our lives over to the care of God
as we understood God.*

Humpty Dumpty sat on a wall,
Humpty Dumpty had a great fall;
All the King's horses, and all the King's men
Cannot put Humpty Dumpty together again!

🍂 WE ALL KNOW THAT HUMPTY DUMPTY'S FALL WAS so great that no one could restore him. The King, his men, the horses, the curious crowd all stood around powerless to help. They could only make futile efforts. But after so much glue and sweat and trouble, it was obvious that nobody could help old Humpty Dumpty. Imagine what they said as they left the scene of the accident: "He was stupid. We could see it coming. He was just teetering on that wall. He was bound to lose his balance and fall one day—I told you so."

Most of us in recovery can identify with Humpty Dumpty. Our lives are the broken pieces that lay scattered all over the sidewalk. We know the looks, the words, the shaking heads, the righteous pronouncements of those who condemn us. But now we know something else. We know there are others not so willing to count us out. These others are part of the recovery community. They have witnessed miracles—miracles in their own lives and in the lives of countless others.

It is this community of the mended and still mending that points us to faith and decision. Through others' testimony, we understand that our Higher Power is worthy of our trust. Our Higher Power can do for us what no one else could do—put us back together again—if we make the decision to trust, to turn.

IN STEP THREE WE COME TO A PLACE OF DECISION, not action. We decide to turn our will and our lives over to the care of God as we are growing to understand God. This decision will, by itself, create a new serenity in our lives, and it will prepare us for the introspective action of Step Four.

Step Three coaxes us to prayerfully declare an attitude of humility and confidence in God's will and control. After we work Step Three for that very important first time, it becomes a daily part of our lives and recovery. In reality, Steps One, Two, and Three become the foundation for our sobriety and sanity. Daily, we turn our will and our lives over to God's care—we have to. For this reason Step Three prayers have a daily flavor to them. We might pray, "God, somehow I know that you can handle my life better than I can. Although it frightens me, I've decided to give you control of my life today."

Third Step Prayer

God, I offer myself to thee, to build with me and to do with me as thou wilt. Relieve me of the bondage of self, that I may better do thy will. Take away my difficulties, that victory over them may bear witness to those I would help of thy Power, thy Love, and thy way of life. May I do thy will always!

My First Prayer

I surrender to you my entire life,
O God of my understanding.
I have made a mess of it
trying to run it myself.
You take it, the whole thing,
and run it for me,
According to your will and plan.

My Daily Prayer

God, I turn my will and my life over to you this day for
your keeping. Your will, Lord, not mine. I ask for
your guidance and direction. I will walk humbly with
you and my fellowman. You are giving me a grateful
heart for my many blessings. You are removing the
defects of character that stand in my way. You are
giving me freedom from self-will.
Let love, compassion, and understanding be in my every
thought, word, and deed this day. I release those to
you who have mistreated me. I truly desire your
abundance of truth, love, harmony, and peace.
As I go out today to do your bidding, let me help anyone
I can who is less fortunate than I.

A Morning Prayer

Good morning, God. You are ushering in another day,
all nice and freshly new.
Here I come again, dear Lord. Please renew me too.

Forgive the many errors that I made yesterday,
and let me come again, dear God, to walk in your own way.
But, God, you know I cannot do it on my own.
Please take my hand and hold it tight, for I cannot walk alone.

Guide Me

Thank you, Higher Power, for this beautiful day, for
    strength, for health.
Help me to live this day for you.
Place in my pathway some way to serve others.
Help me to know that no other walks in my shoes, that
    there is something that only I can do today.
Guide my thoughts and deeds that I may feel your
    presence today and in all the tomorrows.

For Another Day

Thank you, dear God, for another day,
The chance to live in a decent way,
To feel again the joy of living,
And happiness that comes from giving.
Thank you for friends who can understand
And the peace that flows from your loving hand.
Help me to wake to the morning sun
With the prayer, "Today thy will be done,"
For with your help I will find the way.
Thank you again, dear God, for another day.

New Day

Thank you, God, for today. This is the beginning of a new day. I can waste it or use it for good.

What I do today is important because I am exchanging a day of my life for it.

When tomorrow comes, this day will be gone forever — leaving in its place something I have traded for it.

I want it to be gain, not loss; good, not evil; success, not failure; in order that I shall not regret the price I paid for today.

Help Me Remember

Dear Higher Power,
Help me remember that nothing is going to happen to me today that you and I together can't handle.

The Right Road

Dear God,
I have no idea where I am going.
I do not see the road ahead of me.
I cannot know for certain where it will end.
I'm not even sure if I'm on the right road.
But this I believe:
I believe that the desire to please you does, in fact,
    please you.
I hope I have that desire in everything I do.
I hope I never do anything apart from that desire.

And I know that if I do this you will lead me by the right
road, though I may know nothing about it at the time.
Therefore, I will trust you always, for though I may seem
to be lost and in the shadow of death, I will not be
afraid, because I know you will never leave me to face
my troubles alone.

Lead Me and Guide Me

Almighty God, I humbly pray,
Lead me and guide me through this day.
Cast out my selfishness and sin,
Open my heart to let you in.
Help me now as I blindly stray
Over the pitfalls along the way.
Let me have courage to face each task,
Invest me with patience and love, I ask.
Care for me through each hour today,
Strengthen and guard me now, I pray.

As I forgive, forgive me too,
Needing your mercy as I do.
Oh, give me your loving care,
Never abandon me to despair.
Yesterday's wrongs I would seek to right,
Make me more perfect in your sight.
Oh, teach me to live as best I can,
Use me to help my fellowman.
Save me from acts of bitter shame,
    I humbly ask it in your name.

The Lord's Prayer

Our Father, who art in heaven, hallowed be thy Name.
Thy kingdom come.
Thy will be done, on earth as it is in heaven.
Give us this day our daily bread.
And forgive us our trespasses, as we forgive those who
    trespass against us.
And lead us not into temptation, but deliver us from evil.
For thine is the kingdom and the power and the glory,
    forever and ever.

Prayers

f o r

Step Four

4

Made a searching and fearless
moral inventory of ourselves.

🐛 "STOP IT DADDY, YOU'RE HURTING ME," THE LITTLE girl cried.

"I'm gonna hurt you. That's for damn sure," screamed the fierce-eyed man. "Now clean this up." He pushed his daughter toward the spilled orange juice on the floor of the fast-food restaurant. The mother hung her head and bit her lip, but the father continued, "Why are you so damned careless?" Tears now mingled with the juice as the little one on hands and knees blotted her mistake with napkins. "You've ruined breakfast for everyone!" He spit his words as if trying to rid his mouth of a bad taste.

By this time, every eye in the restaurant watched and sympathized for the girl. One man whispered to his wife, "I oughta pour orange juice on that jerk's head," but he only sat and watched. For a while, time stopped for everyone — except the little girl.

Everyone in the restaurant that day, except the father himself, could see his cruelty. As far as we know, there is no happy ending to the story. The father didn't apologize before he left the restaurant; the upset bystander didn't beat some sense into the dad; and the mother didn't stand up for herself and the kids. The little girl believed that her mistake was a serious offense. She believed that she was stupid and clumsy, and she believed that it was all her fault, that she single-handedly ruined breakfast for the entire family. The happy endings only start when our Higher Power helps us take the blinders off and look at our behavior in Step Four.

STEP FOUR ASKS US TO MAKE A SEARCHING AND FEAR-less moral inventory of ourselves. This step does not de-mand that we suddenly change. It is about making a list — period. We learn in the Twelve Steps that the changes — the deep and lasting changes — occur gradually according to our own pace and in God's time.

In this step we search our hearts and lives for those defects, shortcomings, and wrongs that have marked our lives and affected its quality up until this time. Our inven-tory lists more than our defects and shortcomings. It also lists our survival techniques — our dysfunctional attempts at living life on our terms.

Plus, our inventory lists our strengths, which God will transform and use. Yes, Step Four provides for a positive inventory, a list of our positive traits. This is often more difficult than listing our faults.

Step Four begins as we search our hearts in preparing our moral inventory. We begin by asking our Higher Power to search our hearts and show us our weaknesses. God, and most everyone around us, knows our faults; we are the ones who are not up-to-speed. But we cannot change just be-cause someone else points out our defects. It doesn't work that way. Others have been rubbing our noses in our indiscretions for years, and we haven't changed. Only our Higher Power can show us our hearts. Only we can recog-nize the moral defects and make our lists.

We might pray, "God, you know my faults and short-comings better than I do. Show me what you see. Help me recognize my defects, and make a list. But don't just show me what's wrong. Show me what's right, too."

Fourth Step Prayer

Dear God,
   It is I who have made my life a mess. I have done it,
but I cannot undo it. My mistakes are mine, and I will
begin a searching and fearless moral inventory. I will
write down my wrongs, but I will also include that which
is good. I pray for the strength to complete the task.

Light a Candle

O God of my understanding,
Light a candle within my heart,
That I may see what is therein
And remove the wreckage of the past.

To Be Honest

Higher Power, help me to be honest with myself.
It is so easy to alibi, to make excuses for my shortcomings.
It is so easy to blame others and circumstances as a child
      does.
Help me to see myself honestly:
      a human being who needs you this day and every day.
Help me to surrender my weak will to your strength.

I Need to Take a Trip

God, I'm told I need to take a trip—a trip inside myself.
I guess this trip could be pretty hard and very dark.
So I want you to come along and bring your light.
I'm not sure what I'll find; maybe I'll find myself.
I know I'm rough and demanding and always right.
But I'm not sure I'm as rotten as they say.
Maybe I am.
Maybe there's good in there, too; do you think so?
Well, I better start.
You're coming aren't you, God?
I don't want to go in there alone.

My Worth

I pray to remember that my worth is not determined by my show of outward strength, or the volume of my voice, or the thunder of my accomplishments. It is to be seen, rather, in terms of the nature and depth of my commitments, the genuineness of my friendships, the sincerity of my purpose, the quiet courage of my convictions, my capacity to accept life on life's terms, and my willingness to continue "growing up." This I pray.

5

Prayers *f o r* Step Five

---

*Admitted to God, to ourselves,
and to another human being
the exact nature of our wrongs.*

❧ I ONCE ASKED MY FRIEND MARK WHY HE SO seldom spoke of his parents. Mark explained that growing up in his mother's home was nothing to cherish. When pressed, Mark shared an incredible story about a mother who had insanely kept every single piece of trash, even the most vile, for over twenty years. He described a house bursting with clutter and garbage. And he recounted how, when he was thirteen, his mother forced him from the home. Why? Because he had tried to clean his room.

Following his mother's suicide, Mark showed me the house. Once inside the door, we ascended a mountain of trash and walked stooped over, with only a few feet of clearance between the mound and the ceiling. As we crawled through the living room, Mark told me that there was a piano down there somewhere. But I had already discovered enough. I had to escape from the filth. The stench, however, followed me outside. Once in the yard, my legs began to sting. I discovered that my feet, ankles, and lower pant legs were blackened with hundreds of fleas. To say the least, the house was beyond belief and took many weeks to clean.

This story is not unlike our lives. Many of us have allowed habits, resentments, failings, and many other vile things to accumulate in our lives. Our spirits are full of deadly poison. Step Four helped us identify the moral defects, and now Step Five helps us rid ourselves of their stench. Step Five allows the doors to be opened and the wrongs to be aired.

STEP FIVE REQUIRES ADMISSION. WE ADMIT TO GOD, to ourselves, and to another human being the exact nature of the wrongs we listed in Step Four. Our Higher Power aids us in this process that makes us vulnerable, and if we ask for help, we will be directed to the right human being to whom we can admit our wrongs.

It is easy for many of us in recovery to hide in a "just-a-dirty-rotten-person" mode. In this mind-set we may say, "There's no reason to admit specifically—I'm all bad and my whole life is a mess. I'm just a dirty sinner, rotten to the bone."

As long as we see ourselves as all bad, and reveal ourselves only in general, we never begin to deal with the specific hindrances and enduring defects of our lives. We use this attitude as a defense because of our fear—the fear of being vulnerable. In times like this we need our Higher Power's help all the more. Our Higher Power can help us be specific in admitting the exact nature of our wrongs.

Step Five explicitly calls us to admit our wrongs to God. We reveal what we discovered in Step Four. We might pray, "God, give me the honesty and courage to admit what you showed me about myself. Give me another human being to whom I can admit my wrongs. And help me be honest with you and myself. You showed me that I…"

Fifth Step Prayer

Higher Power,

My inventory has shown me who I am, yet I ask for your help in admitting my wrongs to another person and to you. Assure me, and be with me, in this step, for without this step I cannot progress in my recovery. With your help, I can do this, and I will do it.

All That We Ought

All that we ought to have thought and have not thought,
All that we ought to have said and have not said,
All that we ought to have done and have not done;
All that we ought not to have thought and yet have
 thought,
All that we ought not to have spoken and yet have spoken,
All that we ought not to have done and yet have done;

For thoughts, words, and works, pray we, O God, for
 forgiveness,
And with your guidance, seek to change.

Show Me Who

Show me who can hear my confession and not hurt
 me back.
Show me who can stand my story and not condemn.
Show me who can listen and honestly care.

Show me who can be a human being and still show
    mercy.
Show me who can bear to mind my list, which is long.
Show me who can hear the exact nature of my wrongs.

Give Me Courage

God,
I've never had to tell somebody else about my wrongs.
I've never confessed to a priest or even to my dog.
I've kept it all inside and sought to hide.
I've been too frightened to admit what I really am.
Give me courage to tell somebody else what I've found.

6

Prayers

f o r

Step Six

*Were entirely ready to work
in partnership with God
to remove our ineffective behavior.*

❧ THE TAXI DEPOSITED GRANDPA AT THE CURB, and he lumbered toward the house, suitcase in one hand and satchel in the other. Steve kept his eye on the satchel because he knew it held the gifts. This time the satchel offered up a red truck, which Steve took right to the dirt pile. The truck worked hard for several minutes before Steve noticed a missing wheel. No amount of looking turned it up. The wheel had disappeared. Then Grandpa came out to see the toy in action.

Steve was frightened. All he could think about was how his dad would react if he found out. He would slap his head and call him stupid. "Damn you! Get a brain!" he'd say. Dad would shame him for losing something his grandpa had paid good money for.

"How's the truck work, Steve?" Grandpa asked.

"Real good, Grandpa. Thanks." But Steve never looked up. Then Grandpa bent down to show Steve a special feature of the truck, and he noticed the missing wheel. Steve froze.

"Oops, what happened?" Grandpa asked. "Looks like we lost a wheel. Let me help you look for it."

Steve searched his grandfather's face for disappointment or anger, but he found none. He only saw concerned eyes looking for a missing wheel.

Steve feared his benevolent grandfather because his father taught him to fear and to feel shame. But Grandpa wasn't like his dad.

In the same way, we sometimes fear God because of the

abuse of our parents or others. But God is good, and he won't shame or slap or swear. We can grow comfortable with the idea of working with God to remove our ineffective behavior. We don't need to panic. Step Six isn't a time for action yet. It is a time to get ready.

READINESS OR WILLINGNESS IS A STATE OF MIND AND heart, and Step Six acknowledges this. The earlier steps, especially Steps Four and Five, have made us acutely aware of our need to change. And now Step Six gives us the time and opportunity to recognize and collect our readiness to move on to the work of change that still lies ahead.

For many, Step Six can be a time for our emotions to catch up with our experience. The distraction of making an inventory in Step Four and the anxiety of admitting our wrongs in Step Five have kept us active. Step Six requires no action. Instead, we wait upon our Higher Power to produce in us a readiness to move on. Sometimes that readiness comes in the form of sorrow for past wrongs. For the first time perhaps, we've faced ourselves head-on. It's often painful.

In this step it's OK to express our sorrow, regret, and remorse to our Higher Power in prayer. Many of us have damaged the lives of others. Some of us have destroyed and wasted years of our own lives. Many of us have lost, through absence or dysfunction, precious early years of our children's lives. The effects of our character defects have been destructive and painful. It's appropriate to express remorse to God.

But to finish with Step Six business, we move beyond emotional remorse and sorrow. We move, finally, to a place of correct thinking. We want, with clear thought and new willingness, a change: the removal of our defects.

Step Six implicitly acknowledges the presence and work of a Higher Power in our lives who helps us become willing to let go of our defects. Meditation or "listening prayer" is often called for in times like Step Six. We should be cautious not to use many words in Step Six prayers. Instead, we should release our distractions, open ourselves to hear, and quiet ourselves to allow our Higher Power to work.

A Step Six prayer might begin with a plea for our Higher Power to quiet our hearts. The following is an example: "My mind is cluttered, God. Please help. Focus my mind and my heart on the work you're doing inside me. Make me willing to accept the change you're bringing."

Sixth Step Prayer

Dear God,
I am ready for your help in removing from me the defects of character that I now realize are an obstacle to my recovery. Help me to continue being honest with myself and guide me toward spiritual and mental health.

Now

Higher Power,

I don't like what I was.
    But I'm not sure what I am.
I was a liar.

Now I'm numb.
I was a manipulator.
Now I'm frightened of others.
I was a controller.
Now I'm powerless.
I was a bully.
Now I'm my own victim.
I was afraid of pain.
Now I hold pain's hand.
I used to hide in isolation.
Now I'm locked up with you.
I used to be bold and loud.
Now I'm afraid to speak.
I used to think only of myself.
Now I think only about the pain I caused.
I used to trust only in myself.
Now I am in your hands.

O God, I'm ready, please change me.

No Other

I have no other helper than you,
no other father,
no other redeemer,
no other support.
I pray to you.
Only you can help me.
My present misery is too great.
Despair grips me,
and I am at my wits' end.
I am sunk in the depths,
and I cannot pull myself up or out.

If it is your will,
   help me out of this misery.
Let me know that you are stronger than all misery and all
   enemies.
O Lord, if I come through this, please let the experience
   contribute to my and my contemporaries' blessing.
You will not forsake me;
   this I know.

Quiet My Heart

Quiet my heart, God
From all the activity and noise.
Help me center my thoughts, my mind.
Remove the distractions that spin me.
My wrongs, my faults lie before you.
You know me inside out, the good and the bad.
Help me receive your inner working and change.
I want to turn my back on yesterday's ways.
I want to truly desire change, lasting change.
So quiet my heart, make me ready.

7

Prayers

f o r

Step Seven

*Humbly asked God to help us
remove our shortcomings.*

❦ HE ALWAYS COMES LATE TO THE MEETING. HE misses the reading time and never seems to listen to others. He can't wait until he can talk. He tells us how awful his wife is and how sick he is. He is so persecuted and down-trodden—pathetic. No one at work understands his struggles. And if he should slip and come to a meeting with alcohol on his breath...well. "Who can blame me?" he asks. His litany of complaints takes an eternity to recite. And we're all supposed to feel sorry for him.

In our addiction, many of us exercise a false humility that is designed to elicit grace and sympathy from others—even from God. We try to make people feel sorry for us. "We weren't dealt a fair hand in life! It's not our fault if we fail! We were doomed to fail. Our fate made it so!" And so our unfortunate circumstances in life give us the right to feel sorry for ourselves and to expect special treatment from others—*not!*

This addictive insanity is not humility. Our Higher Power doesn't give favor because we manipulate to get it. God gives grace to the humble because they freely admit their needs and trust a power greater than themselves for the answers. Many of us have lived years getting what we want through manipulation, but it won't work with God. Humility obtains God's favor, and surrender gains God's approval.

Humility is a state of mind and heart. But more, it is the spirit and attitude that controls the rest of our way out, our spiritual journey, a journey that humbly relies upon our Higher Power and that humbly faces our shortcomings. In Step Seven we come to God, not to confess and not to change. We tried to change, we determined to do better, but we always failed. Now it is time to ask, to humbly ask God to help us remove what we cannot remove ourselves: our shortcomings.

STEP SEVEN IS A SPECIFIC CALL FOR PRAYER AS WE humbly ask our Higher Power to help us remove our shortcomings. Steps Four, Five, and Six have prepared us for this prayer and this step. We are humbled before God and anxious for right standing before our Higher Power. We might pray, "God, I see my shortcomings, and I know my powerlessness over my faults. I have truly had a change of heart and mind as far as my old ways are concerned. I want you to take them away, please. I cannot change on my own — I know that now. But you can help me change. Please do."

Seventh Step Prayer

My Creator,
    I am willing that you should have all of me, good and bad. I pray that you now help me to remove every single defect of character that stands in the way of my usefulness to you and my fellowman. Grant me strength as I go out from here to do your bidding.

Who, Me?

I need to be forgiven, Lord,
    so many times a day.
So often do I stumble and fall.
    Be merciful, I pray.
Help me not be critical
    when others' faults I see.
For so often, Lord,
    the same faults are in me.

Enough to Need

Dear God, never allow me to think that I have
    knowledge enough to need no teaching,
    wisdom enough to need no correction,
    talents enough to need no grace,
    goodness enough to need no progress,
    humility enough to need no repentance,
    devotion enough to need no improvement,
    strength sufficient without your spirit,
lest, standing still, I fall back forevermore.

Prayer for Healing

Higher Power,
    You have told us to ask and we will receive, to seek
and we will find, to knock and you will open the door
to us.
    I trust in your love for me and in the healing power

of your compassion. I praise you and thank you for the mercy you have shown to me.

Higher Power, I am sorry for all my mistakes. I ask for your help in removing the negative patterns of my life. I accept with all my heart your forgiving love.

And I ask for the grace to be aware of the character defects that exist within myself. Let me not offend you by my weak human nature or by my impatience, resentment, or neglect of people who are a part of my life. Rather, teach me the gift of understanding and the ability to forgive, just as you continue to forgive me.

I seek your strength and your peace so that I may become your instrument in sharing those gifts with others.

Guide me in my prayer that I might know what needs to be healed and how to ask you for that healing.

It is you, Higher Power, whom I seek. Please enter the door of my heart and fill me with the presence of your spirit now and forever.

I thank you, God, for doing this.

True Power

Take from me, Higher Power,
   my false pride and grandiosity,
   all my phoniness and self-importance,
And help me find
   the courage that shows itself in gentleness,
   the wisdom that shows itself in simplicity, and
   the true power that shows itself in modesty and humility

Humility Prayer

Lord, I am far too much influenced by what people
think of me, which means that I am always pretending
to be either richer or smarter than I really am.

Please prevent me from trying to attract attention.
Don't let me gloat over praise on the one hand and be
discouraged by criticism on the other, nor let me waste
time weaving the most imaginary situations in which the
heroic, charming, witty person present is myself.

Show me how to be humble of heart.

Release Me

Lord, keep me from the habit of thinking I must
say something on every subject and on every occasion.

Release me from wanting to control everybody's
affairs. Keep my mind free from the recital of endless
details—give me wings to get to the point.

I ask for grace enough to listen to the tales of others'
pains. Help me to endure them with patience, but seal my
lips on my own aches and pains—they are increasing and
my love of rehearsing them is becoming sweeter as the
years go by.

Teach me the glorious lesson that occasionally it is
possible that I may be mistaken.

Keep me reasonably sweet. I do not want to be a
saint—some of them are so hard to live with—but a sour
old person is one of the crowning works of the devil.

Give me the ability to see good things in unexpected places and talents in unexpected people. And give me, O Lord, the grace to tell them so.

Make me thoughtful, but not moody; helpful, but not bossy. With my vast store of wisdom, it seems a pity not to use it all, but you know, Lord, that I want a few friends at the end.

Right Living

Higher Power, deliver me:
   From the cowardice that dare not face new truth,
   From the laziness that is contented with half-truth,
   From the arrogance that thinks it knows all truth.
These things, good Lord, that I pray for,
   Give me the strength to work for.

Do the Right Thing

Help me, Higher Power, to get out of myself, to stop always thinking what I need. Show me the way I can be helpful to others, and supply me with the strength to do the right thing.

8

Prayers *f o r* Step Eight

Made a list of all persons we had
harmed and became willing
to make amends to them all.

❦ CARL WAS FIRED FROM EVERY JOB HE EVER HAD—
some twenty-one jobs. Some jobs only lasted a few days.
His longest lasted eighteen months. Carl told how he always
lost his jobs because someone else didn't understand him.
Bosses asked for too much, fellow workers took advantage
of him, or the jobs were too hard for too little pay. It never
was his fault, always someone else's. He finally moved north
to greener pastures.

Carl once told me that his father regularly and severely
beat him with a strap. Carl said he left home at the age of
seventeen to escape the punishment. Somehow I wasn't
surprised when I saw Carl's teenage daughter attending a
Twelve-Step group for youth. She had run away from Carl's
greener pastures and traveled six hundred miles on her own
to live with her aunt. The girl spoke tearfully of her dad and
said, "He's never wrong! It's always my fault!"

So long as we judge and evaluate the defects and shortcomings of others, we never have to face our own. It's time
now, in Step Eight, to think about the people we have hurt,
not to blame them.

STEP EIGHT PROVIDES A TIME FOR REFLECTION. LIKE
Step Six, it is a time to recognize and collect our willingness
to move on. But unlike Step Six, Step Eight calls for action.
It asks us to make a list of the persons we have harmed. As
the names and faces of friends, family, enemies, associates,
and others come before us, we must be ever vigilant to

remember that the program is about us, not them. Many of the people whom we recall and list have hurt and damaged us, too. But we are working our program, not theirs. If we ask, our Higher Power helps us see these people from God's perspective, not ours.

Step Eight provides an opportunity for acknowledging the presence and work of our Higher Power in our lives. "Listening prayer" is again called for as we allow our Higher Power to bring to mind the names and faces of those whom we have harmed. Once we have prayed for God's help in making our list, we need to listen for God's voice and direction.

Prayers for Step Eight might say, "O God, I know I have harmed others along the way. Help me recall the names and faces of those to whom you would have me make amends. Quiet my heart, center my thoughts on hearing your voice. Keep me from recalling the pain others have caused me. Help me take responsibility."

Eighth Step Prayer

Higher Power,

I ask your help in making my list of all those I have harmed. I will take responsibility for my mistakes and be forgiving to others as you are forgiving to me. Grant me the willingness to begin my restitution. This I pray.

Open Mind

Higher Power, may I understand how:
To be alert to my own needs, not to the faults of others;
To remain teachable;
To listen;
To keep an open mind; and
To learn not who's right but what's right.

It's About Me

Help me remember, God, that this program is about me. I find myself wanting to judge and blame and accuse everyone but myself. I'm supposed to be making a list of all those I have harmed, yet my mind is full of those who have offended me. Is this some sort of mental defense mechanism to keep myself from facing the pain I've caused others?

Help me get over this stumbling block. I release those who hurt me. I forgive. I put those people in your hands, God. Vengeance is yours. Wait God...don't punish them. I'm just as guilty...don't punish me.

Help me make things right.

9

Prayers

f o r

Step Nine

Made direct amends to such people
wherever possible, except when to do so
would injure them or others.

❦ THE RECORDING BOOTH ENGINEER HELPED me make a radio spot that mentioned God. When it was done, she told me, "You know, I could never be religious. My mother forever ruined me." She spoke with rigid defiance. Her lip curled when she said, "My mother."

When I asked why, she explained how her mother belonged to a particular religious sect that didn't allow birthday celebrations, Christmas observances, or even flag salutes. She hissed in anger as she remembered her humiliation at being told to leave the classroom during the morning pledge of allegiance. Then she quieted her voice as she recalled her mother's absence at her wedding and at the birth of her daughter.

"She punished me," she said, "because I had rejected her faith. I haven't seen her in seven years. And I'm not sure if I want to see her."

Just like this woman, many of us in recovery find it hard to approach certain people in our lives because of past offenses. And we may never feel free so long as there are things that need to be made right. We can't make their offenses right, but we can take responsibility for ourselves and make amends for our harmful behavior. That's all we're supposed to do.

When we actually begin the process of making amends, we may go back to people we have hurt and find that they are unwilling to accept our amends, but that's OK. Our Higher Power knows we have tried. The woman above may one day seek to make things right with her mother and her mother may still reject her. But the God we are getting to know will honor her attempt.

STEP NINE CALLS FOR ACTION. IT ALSO CALLS FOR courage. Many agree that this is the most difficult step, but many *also* agree that it is the most powerful step. Step Nine allows us to make a significant and lasting break from our past behavior. Step Nine enables us to separate ourselves from the mistakes of our past. This step is for us—first and foremost.

Although Step Nine doesn't specifically call for prayer, its very nature hurls us headlong into prayer. We complain to our Higher Power as we air our fears and resistance. We appeal for courage as we face people we'd rather not face. We pray for strength to endure the rejection we might find. We ask for help to withstand the pressure without seeking out our former addictions.

We might pray, "God, I'm scared to face some of these people to whom I must make amends. In fact, God, I've spent a great deal of effort avoiding most of those on my list. Give me courage to face these people and this step. Let this step help me put the past behind."

Ninth Step Prayer

Higher Power,
I pray for the right attitude to make my amends, being ever mindful not to harm others in the process.

I ask for your guidance in making indirect amends. Most important, I will continue to make amends by staying abstinent, helping others, and growing in spiritual progress.

Life Is a Celebration

Lord, help me today to:
Mend a quarrel.
Seek out a forgotten friend.
Dismiss suspicion and replace it with trust.
Write a friendly letter.
Share a treasure.
Give a soft answer.
Encourage another.
Manifest my loyalty in word and deed.
Keep a promise.
Find the time.
Forego a grudge.
Forgive an enemy.
Listen.
Acknowledge any wrongdoing.
Try to understand.
Examine my demands on others.
Think of someone else first.
Be kind.
Be gentle.
Laugh a little.
Smile more.
Be happy.
Show my gratitude.
Welcome a stranger.
Speak your love.

Speak it again.
Live it again.
Life is a celebration!

Finish the Business

Higher Power,

Step Nine is a way for me to finish the business that
has been left undone for so long. For many years I have
taken no thought for the damage I was doing through my
abuse.

I have stolen that which was not mine.

I have broken promises that were meant to last a
lifetime.

I have wounded spirits that may never be healed.

I have lost the trust of precious friends and family.

I have used others for my own purpose.

I have lost precious years with loved ones.

I know that you have forgiven me, Higher Power.
You accept me. Now help me reach out in sincerity to
these. I cannot change the past. I cannot relive the
wasted years. But with your help I can say I'm sorry, I
can show I've changed, I can finish the business.

Excuses

God, help me stop making excuses and start making
amends. You've heard me say:

I needn't look for this one 'cause he's probably dead.

I don't have to make amends to them, they hurt me
more.

I won't call this guy, he wouldn't remember.
I can't talk to him, he'll explode.
I'll never reach out to her, she's a gossip.
I can't bear the pain of seeing this one...
No, it won't work...I can't...this is too hard...

Have you heard me make the excuses, God? I used to think I had guts. I used to think I had courage—I don't. Please, God, give me yours.

Help me stop making excuses and start making amends.

10

Prayers

f o r

Step Ten

Continued to take personal inventory and, when we were wrong, promptly admitted it.

🍎 OVER THE YEARS, THE STORIES OF MANY OF MY experiences have taken on legendary proportion. I have spun more imagination that truth into some of the tales. That's okay, I suppose, when I'm telling the kids a bedtime story, but I've noticed that I change history a bit when I talk to adults.

When I did my Step Four inventory, this problem of lying became apparent to me. I realized then that I stretch the truth for a number of reasons. I want others to think better of me. I want to keep myself out of trouble. Or I prefer the less painful lie over the brutal truth. Although I faced my lying problem then, I've learned that old ways die hard.

I was on jury duty recently, and during the time when the lawyers questioned the potential jurors for the trial, they began to ask me questions about my past. I was scared to death because I knew I was under oath to tell the truth. I had to think hard with each question to make sure that my answer was the truth and not an exaggeration. With the help of my Higher Power, I told the truth. I also got stuck with the trial.

This process of keeping one's self in check is what Step Ten is all about. I've realized that I need the continual inventory that Step Ten suggests. Lying or exaggerating is just one of the many defects that continue to pop up from time to time. The program helps me stay on top of these lingering defects through the regular process of taking inventory.

STEP TEN IS THE FIRST OF THE MAINTENANCE STEPS. It begins to teach us a way of life that keeps us from falling back into past mistakes or old habit patterns.

Step Ten encourages us to examine ourselves daily, and it encourages us to make prompt admissions and amends. The prompt recognition, admission, and correction of our behavior helps us maintain a lifestyle that supports recovery and health.

Step Ten reminds us of our need to be willing to change and amend our behavior. These prayers support our desire for change. We ask our Higher Power's help in searching our lives as we seek help and grace to make daily restitutions. We might pray, "God, help me see my life and actions today through your eyes. Show me where I have fallen short. Show me your loving way and help me make things right."

❦   ❦   ❦

Tenth Step Prayer

I pray I may continue:
To grow in understanding and effectiveness;
To take daily spot-check inventories of myself;
To correct mistakes when I make them;
To take responsibility for my actions;
To be ever aware of my negative and self-defeating
    attitudes and behaviors;
To keep my willfulness in check;
To always remember I need your help;
To keep love and tolerance of others as my code; and
To continue in daily prayer how I can best serve you,
    my Higher Power.

"To Be" Prayer

O Lord, I ain't what I ought to be,
And I ain't what I want to be,
And I ain't what I'm going to be,
But, O Lord, I thank you
That I ain't what I used to be.

Run the Race

Help me this day, Higher Power, to run with patience
    the race that is set before me.
May neither opposition without nor discouragement
    within divert me from my progress in recovery.

Inspire in me strength of mind, willingness, and
    acceptance, that I may meet all fears and difficulties
    with courage, and may complete the tasks set before
    me today.

First Things First

Dear Higher Power, remind me:
To tidy up my own mind,
To keep my sense of values straight,
To sort out the possible and the impossible,
To turn the impossible over to you,
And get busy on the possible.

I Promise Myself!

Today I pray:
To promise myself to be so strong that nothing can
    disturb my peace of mind.
To talk health, happiness, and prosperity to every
    person I meet.
To make all my friends feel that there is something in
    them.
To look at the sunny side of everything and make my
    optimism come true.
To think only of the best, to work only for the best, and
    expect only the best.
To be just as enthusiastic about the success of others as
    I am about my own.
To forget the mistakes of the past and press on to the
    greater achievements of the future.

To wear a cheerful countenance at all times and give
every living creature I meet a smile.
To give so much time to the improvement of myself that
I have no time to criticize others.
To be too large for worry, too noble for anger, too strong
for fear, and too happy to permit the presence of
trouble.

Recovery Prayer

Lord, today and every day, I will be ever mindful
that recovery is the most important thing in my life,
without exception. I may believe my job, or my home
life, or one of many other things, comes first. But if I
don't stay with the program, chances are I won't have
a job, a family, sanity, or even life. If I am convinced
that everything in life depends on my recovery, I have
a much better chance of improving my life. If I put
other things first, I am only hurting my chances.

O God of Our Understanding

This is the dawn of a new day in the program. I shall
thank you, my Higher Power, for last night's rest, your
gift.
Yesterday is gone, except for what I have learned
from it, good or bad. Today, I have the same choice, a
divine privilege that swells my heart with hope and
purpose. This is my day, the purity of a new beginning.
I will receive from this day exactly what I give to it.
As I do good things, good will be done to me. It is my gift

to mold into something everlasting and do those things that will affect the people around me in an ever-widening circle. The worthiness of this effort rests entirely with me.

This is my day for love, because I know that as I love, I will be loved. Hate and jealousy cannot exist in the presence of love. I will be sustained by this miracle of your creation and this day will be lightened by my love for others and especially love for my fellow travelers in the program.

Today I will do my best without thought of failures of the past or anxieties for the future. When this day is ended, I will have no regrets. On retiring I shall thank you, my Higher Power, for this wonderful day.

To Change

I pray that I may continue to change, and I appreciate you for investing in me your time, your patience, your understanding and for seeing in me someone worthwhile. I am sorry for the past—but I will change for the better, and I am grateful for the opportunity!

11

Prayers

f o r

Step Eleven

---

*Sought through prayer and meditation
to improve our conscious contact with
God as we understood God, praying
only for knowledge of God's will for us
and for the power to carry that out.*

❦ SAM AND CHARLES WERE EXCITED TO BE ABOARD ship in Pearl Harbor. On one of their first liberty days, they decided to go to Sandy Beach on Oahu, which is famous for bodysurfing.

They put their clothes, valuables, and glasses in a locker and blindly headed for the water. They were confused that such a large crowd had gathered on the sand but so few people were actually in the water. They both squinted, but seeing no apparent reason, the pair entered the water. They had no sooner gotten wet when a loudspeaker blared, "Will you two guys get out of the water? We are trying to hold a bodysurfing contest here!"

When Sam and Charles finally recovered their glasses and their self-respect, they beheld ABC Television cameras, the judges, and the spectators. Oops!

Like the voice over the loudspeaker, our Higher Power instructs us in the way we should walk. People often say that God speaks in a still, small voice. But most of us hear it loud and clear most of the time. God uses pain, meetings, sponsors, counselors, judges, spouses, kids, friends, mistakes, books, and more to get the message across. We don't always listen and obey, but we do hear.

When God points out the way to us, we ought not be embarrassed. We should respond, "Thank you for helping us see life a little more clearly."

STEP ELEVEN IS ALL ABOUT HEARING GOD BETTER. IT IS another maintenance step, and it ensures that we keep in touch with our Higher Power. We develop prayer, meditation, and a God-consciousness that help control our daily living. We understand that God is not there to be manipulated or controlled. Prayer is not our opportunity to tell God how to run our lives or the world. Prayer is a time to connect with our Higher Power who already has a wonderful plan for our lives. It is our job to ask what that plan is and to ask for the strength to accomplish God's will.

Step Eleven explicitly calls for the sort of prayerful petition and spiritual meditation that draws us into fellowship and contact with our Higher Power and into knowledge of God's will for us. We might pray, "God, show me what your will is for me today. I admit that doing your will and not mine is sometimes scary. So I pray that you will also give me the courage and ability to carry out your plan, not mine."

Eleventh Step Prayer

Higher Power, as I understand you,
I pray to keep my connection with you open and clear from the confusion of daily life. Through my prayers and meditations I ask especially for freedom from self-will, rationalization, and wishful thinking. I pray for the guidance of correct thought and positive action. Your will, Higher Power, not mine, be done.

Peace in God's Will

My Higher Power,

Quicken my spirit and fix my thoughts on your will, that
I may see what you would have done, and contemplate its
doing
  without self-consciousness or inner excitement,
  without haste and without delay,
  without fear of other people's judgments, and
  without anxiety about success.
Knowing only that it is your will and therefore must be
done quietly, faithfully, and lovingly, for in your will
alone is my peace.

On Awakening

God, please direct my thinking, especially move it
from self-pity, dishonesty, and self-seeking motives.
As I go through the day and face indecision, please
give me inspiration, an intuitive thought, or a decision.
Make me relax and take it easy; don't let me struggle.
Let me rely upon *your* inspiration, intuitive thoughts,
and decisions instead of my old ideas.
Show me all through the day what my next step is
to be and give me whatever I need to take care of each
problem. God, I ask you especially for freedom from
self-will, and I make no requests for myself only. But
give me the knowledge of your will for me and the power
to carry it out in every contact during the day.

As I go through this day, let me pause when agitated or doubtful and ask you for the right thought or action. Let me constantly be reminded that I am no longer running the show, humbly saying many times each day, "Thy will be done" and agreeing that it is.

I will then be in much less danger of excitement, fear, anger, worry, self-pity, or foolish decisions. I will be more efficient. I won't be burning up energy foolishly as I was when trying to run life to suit myself. I will let you discipline me in this simple way. I will give you all the power and all the praise.

Teach Me

Teach me, God, so that I might know
The way to change and the way to grow.
Give me the words to ask you how
To handle the here and live in the now.
Tempt me not with the valleys of death,
Give me freedom from fear in every breath.
And though mistakes I make in my daily life,
Deliver me from aiding strife.
Understand me God, as I am now,
And show me the furrows I need to plow
To reach my goal as a ripening food,
So I might feed others all that is good.
Fill me with energy known as the power,
Till I come to rest at the midnight hour.

Eternal God

Eternal God,
We know you forgive our trespasses
If we forgive ourselves and others.
We know you protect us from destructive temptation
If we continue to seek your help and guidance.
We know you provide us food and shelter today
If we but place our trust in you
And try to do our best.
Give us this day knowledge of your will for us
And the power to carry it out.
For yours is Infinite Power and Love, forever.

What Is Best

O Lord, you know what is best for me. Let this or that be
done, as you please. Give what you will, how much you
will, and when you will.

Prayer to Know

Grant it to me, Higher Power:
    To know that which is worth knowing,
    To love that which is worth loving,
    To praise that which pleases you most,
    To work for that which helps others.
Grant it to me:
    To distinguish with true judgment things that differ,
        and above all…
    To search out, and to do what is well pleasing to you.

Every Morning

Every morning I will rest my arms a while upon the windowsill of faith, gaze upon my Higher Power, and with that vision in my heart, turn strong to meet my day.

God's Answer

I asked you, God, for strength that I might achieve;
    I was made weak that I might learn humbly to obey.
I asked for help that I might do greater things;
    I was given infirmity that I might do better things.
I asked for riches that I might be happy;
    I was given poverty that I might be wise.
I asked for power that I might have the praise of others;
    I was given weakness that I might feel the need for
    you.
I asked for all things that I might enjoy life;
    I was given life that I might enjoy all things.
No, dear Lord, I've gotten nothing that I asked for
But everything I had hoped for.
Despite myself, my prayers were answered,
And I am among those most richly blessed.

Language of the Heart

Dear God,
You know my needs before I ask,
    my heart before I pray, and
    my gratitude before I even offer my thanks.

You understand me better than I understand myself, and I thank you for communicating with me in the language of the heart.

12

Prayers *f o r* Step Twelve

---

*Having had a spiritual awakening
as the result of these steps,
we tried to carry this message to others,
and to practice these principles
in all our affairs.*

❦ CHELESE TEACHES FIRST GRADE IN AN ILLINOIS public school. School policy doesn't allow her to speak openly of her faith in her Higher Power, but she is not hindered in her ability to show her faith. Last year she had a particularly difficult class because of one boy, Jeff. Jeff lived with only his mom, and she could not help him with homework because she could not read. Chelese was unable to communicate with the mother because Jeff's home had no phone, and the notes that went home came back unopened, unread.

Things would not have been so bad if Jeff had been a reasonably normal boy, but he was not. He was a severe discipline problem, often disrupting the whole class. His fits of anger were so intense that Chelese had to physically restrain Jeff to keep him from destroying the classroom and hurting himself. As she held him tightly, she would say over and over, "I love you, Jeff. You're a good boy. I love you, Jeff."

Chelese could have dumped Jeff on someone else. She could have even had him removed from the small, rural school and bused many miles to an alternative school for discipline problems. But she felt that God wanted him in her class. So she kept him. Jeff threw many fits throughout the year. In return he received many hugs, affirmations, and "I love you's."

On the last day of school, Jeff came late. He walked to school every morning, and on this last day he picked something up along the way. He approached Chelese's desk with a geranium plant behind his back—roots and all. "Here Teacher," he said as he thrust his gift forward, "I love you, too."

STEP TWELVE IS WHEN WE REALIZE THAT THROUGH all these steps, God has been loving us, helping us, and restoring us. Our realization is a spiritual awakening. Not only do we express our love for our Higher Power, but we also carry what we have learned to others who are still struggling, hurting, and living life on their own terms. And then we continue the program in our own lives through the daily practice of the steps. We demonstrate the principles of the program every day.

Step Twelve prayers are requests for commitment as we practice the program in our daily lives and share it with others. Again, courage is important and something we should pray for. We might pray, "God, show me how I can best share the program with others. Give me courage to reach out. Help me not to judge. Keep me ever mindful that this program is a way of life and that I need to practice it in my everyday living."

🌱　🌱　🌱

Twelfth Step Prayer

Dear God,
My spiritual awakening continues to unfold. The help I have received I shall pass on and give to others, both in and out of the fellowship. For this opportunity I am grateful.

I pray most humbly to continue walking day by day on the road of spiritual progress. I pray for the inner strength and wisdom to practice the principles of this way of life in all I do and say. I need you, my friends, and the program every hour of every day. This is a better way to live.

Thank You, God

Thank you, God, for all you have given me.
Thank you for all you have taken from me.
But, most of all, I thank you, God, for what you've left
    me:
Recovery, along with peace of mind, faith, hope, and love.

The Gratitude Prayer

O God,
I want to thank you for bringing me this far along the
    road to recovery.
It is good to be able to get my feet on the floor again.
It is good to be able to do at least some things for myself
    again.
It is best of all just to have the joy of feeling well again.

O God,
Keep me grateful;
Grateful to all the people who helped me back to health;
Grateful to you for the way in which you have brought
    me through it all.

O God,
Still give me patience.
Help me not to be in too big a hurry to do too much.
Help me to keep on doing what I'm told to do.
Help me to be so obedient to those who know what is
    best for me, that very soon I shall be on the top of the
    world and on the top of my job again.
I can say what the psalmist said:
I waited patiently for the Lord;
He inclined to me and heard my cry.
He took me from a fearful pit, and from the miry clay,
And on a rock he set my feet, establishing my way.

Your Gift

Thank you, Higher Power, for your gift of recovery;
through this program I have come to know myself better
than ever before, and I have come to know others better
as well. I pray that I may be eternally grateful for this,
your blessing!

Unselfishness Prayer

Higher Power, guide me as I walk the narrow way between being selfish and unselfish. I know I must be selfish, to concentrate on my own recovery, so I do not slip
and be of no use to myself or anyone else. Yet I must also
be unselfish, reaching out to others, sensitive to their
needs, and willing to meet them at any time. With your
help, I can do both, and keep a balance that will give me
a right perspective in my life.

Please, Lord

Please, Lord, teach us to laugh again; but God, don't ever let us forget that we cried.

Do It Now

Dear God,

I expect to pass through this world but once.

Any good thing, therefore, that I can do, or any kindness I can show to any fellow traveler, let me do it now.

Let me not defer nor neglect it, for I shall not pass this way again.

The Twelve Steps Prayer

Power, greater than myself, as I understand you,
I willingly admit that without your help, I am powerless
    over my dependencies and my life has become
    unmanageable.
I believe you can restore me to wholeness.
I turn my life and my will over to you.
I have made a searching and fearless moral inventory of
    myself;
I admit to you, to myself, and to another the exact nature
    of my wrongs.
I am entirely ready to work in partnership with you to
    remove my ineffective behavior.
I humbly ask you to help me remove my shortcomings.
I have made direct amends to all persons I have harmed,
    except when to do so would injure them or others.

I will continue to take personal inventory, and when I
    am wrong, I will promptly admit it.
I seek through prayer and meditation to improve my
    conscious contact with you and pray only for
    knowledge of your will for me and for the power to
    carry it out.
Grant me the grace to carry the message of your help
    unto others and to practice the principles of the
    Twelve Steps in all my affairs.

No Greater Power

To find direction and meaning I must tap a Higher
Power. That's you, Lord, as I understand you. I will start
each day with God and take Steps Three, Seven, and
Eleven. There is no Greater Power. And then I will pray:
Lord, I turn my life and will over to you today.
I will walk humbly with you and my fellow travelers.
You are giving me a grateful heart for my many blessings.
You are directing my thinking and separating me from
    self-pity, dishonesty, and self-seeking motives.
You are removing my resentments, fears, and other
    character defects that stand in my way.
You are giving me freedom from self-will.
Your will, Lord, not mine.
You will show me today what I can do to help someone
    who is still hurting.
As I go out today to do your bidding,
You are helping me to become a better person.

Possibilities Prayer

I know, dear God, that my part in this program is going
to be a thrilling and endless adventure. Despite all that
has happened to me already, I know that I have just
begun to grow. I have just begun to open to your love.
I have just begun to touch the varied lives you are using
me to change. I have just begun to sense the possibilities
ahead. And these possibilities, I am convinced, will
continue to unfold into ever new and richer adventures,
not only for the rest of my reborn days but through
eternity.

Things to Give

Today, I pray I may give:

To my enemy: Forgiveness.
To my opponent: Tolerance.
To my customer: Service.
To a friend: Kindness.
To all people: Charity.
To my family: My heart.
To every child: A good example.
To myself: Respect.
To you, Higher Power: *Love* With all my heart,
                      With all my soul,
                      With all my mind.

Prayer of Saint Francis of Assisi

Lord, make me an instrument of your peace!
Where there is hatred, let me sow love.
Where there is injury, pardon.
Where there is doubt, faith.
Where there is despair, hope.
Where there is darkness, light.
Where there is sadness, joy.
O Divine Master, grant that I may not so much seek
    To be consoled as to console.
    To be understood as to understand.
    To be loved as to love.
For it is in giving that we receive.
It is in pardoning that we are pardoned.
It is in dying that we are born to eternal life.

Anniversary Prayer

Dear God, I had another anniversary today, one more
year in recovery. It has been difficult at times, but it has
allowed many blessings. I am a human being again. I feel
new strength in my body, spirit, and mind. The world has
never looked so good. I have my friends' and family's respect. I am productive in my work. I do not miss the slip-
pery people and places. When I have been tempted, you,
my Higher Power, have sustained me. I have found a
home in the fellowship, and friends support me. Stay
close by me, God. I thank you. *This is the life I love.*

The Twelve Rewards

Spirit of God,
I humbly ask for your help, so I may continue to realize
the rewards of recovery:
1. Hope instead of desperation.
2. Faith instead of despair.
3. Courage instead of fear.
4. Peace of mind instead of confusion.
5. Self-respect instead of self-contempt.
6. Self-confidence instead of helplessness.
7. The respect of others instead of pity and contempt.
8. A clean conscience instead of a sense of guilt.
9. Real friendship instead of loneliness.
10. A clean pattern of life instead of a purposeless
    existence.
11. The love and understanding of my family instead of
    doubts and fears.
12. The freedom of a happy life instead of the bondage
    of addiction.

Sobriety Prayer

If I speak in the tongues of people and even of
angels, but have not sobriety, I am a noisy gong or a
clanging cymbal. And if I have prophetic powers and
understand all mysteries and all knowledge, and if I
have all faith so as to move mountains, but have not
sobriety, I am nothing. If I give away all that I have,
and if I deliver my body to be burned, but have not
sobriety, I gain nothing.

When I am sober, I am patient and kind. When
I am sober, I am not jealous or boastful, or arrogant,

or rude. When I am sober, I do not insist on my own way. When I am sober, I am not irritable or resentful. I do not rejoice at wrong as I used to do but rejoice in what is right. When I am sober, I can bear all things, believe in all things, hope all things, and endure all things. Sobriety never ends and never fails.

When I was using, I spoke like an arrogant child, thought like a stubborn child, and reasoned like a rebellious child. When I chose sobriety for my life, I gave up my childish ways.

So faith, hope, love, and sobriety abide, but for me, the most important has to be sobriety, for without it, I cannot have the other three, nor can I ever have the serenity I yearn to possess.

13

The Serenity Prayer

God, grant me
the serenity to accept
the things I cannot change;
the courage to change the things I can;
and the wisdom to know the difference.

❦ SOME PARENTS GOT THE FOLLOWING LETTER FROM their little angel who was away at college:

Dear Mom and Dad,

I hope to make it home for the holidays if they will let me out of the hospital. I was in a car accident in this guy's car. I've wanted to tell you about him ever since I left the dorm to be with him, but the opportunity never arose. As soon as he's out of jail, I'd like you to meet him. He really is a wonderful guy when he's sober, and I think he'll make a great father for the baby especially if he finishes the rehabilitation program.

I hope to go back to school as soon as I can appeal the dean's disciplinary action and raise enough money to buy back my books and computer.

Please don't worry about the car accident; the doctors say I'll be walking again in no time.

Love,
Your Daughter

P.S. Everything in the letter is untrue, but I really do need a hundred dollars, and I did get a "D" in English.

Like the college student who wrote this letter, we who are in recovery have spent many years becoming expert at manipulating and controlling others. We have become masters at trying to change everyone and everything around us to suit our purposes. Rather than living life on life's terms, we have spent years making life conform to our terms. The problem is that it doesn't work. Oh yes, we have lived in the illusion that it is working, but one day the illusion fades, and we are faced with realities that refuse to submit to our control anymore: the rent finally must be paid; the companion finally leaves; the judge isn't interested in explanations; our bodies refuse to go on.

The Serenity Prayer by Reinhold Niebuhr is so popular among the recovery community because it focuses on the most important issue of our recovery: control. The prayer underscores acceptance and serenity rather than manipulation and pressure. It emphasizes responsibility and courage rather than neglect and avoidance. It asks for wisdom and knowledge instead of divine compliance and self-gratification.

This prayer is uniquely suited for the Twelve-Step program. Although Niebuhr was personally unrelated to any Twelve-Step program, his prayer, which was originally written for use in a sermon and, later, published in the *New York Herald Tribune*, became accepted and used by program members the world over. In fact, the prayer in its short form has become known by many as the A.A. prayer.

The first petition, *"God, grant me the serenity to accept the things I cannot change,"* reminds us that there are things in life over which we are not intended to have control. And it asks God for the serenity of heart and mind to understand and accept this truth.

The petition, *"The courage to change the things I can,"* urges us toward action on things we can change. But the petition is for courage—the courage and help that only our Higher Power can provide.

"The wisdom to know the difference" helps us admit that we don't always know what we should accept and what we

should change. This petition reminds us that our weakness is only an opportunity for God to provide us with wisdom.

"Living one day at a time" is an important principle in recovery. Few of us can decide to change our behavior for a lifetime, but we can choose to follow the program today. No Twelve-Step program can guarantee success for tomorrow, but it can offer a way to live today.

The petition, *"Enjoying one moment at a time,"* has a foreign and unfamiliar word to many of us in recovery: *enjoying.* Enjoyment has not marked our life up until now. Childhood was interrupted for many of us. We had to assume adult responsibility or endure adult pain when we should have been playing in joyful abandonment. We can't really enjoy life, but we can seize a moment and choose to enjoy a moment. And then, with God's help, we can string those moments together into some measure of life and happiness.

"Accepting hardship as the pathway to peace" is a very important petition as it prayerfully reminds us that hardship is a part of life. But hardship, like pain, can lead us to serenity. Hardship and pain call our attention to something that is not exactly right in our life or body. Hardship, like pain, is a warning. To acknowledge pain, to accept hardship is to take the hand of our best teacher. Hardship will help us face our lingering dysfunction if we will submit to it.

"Taking, as you did, this sinful world as it is, not as I would have it." This talks about living life on life's terms. But more, Niebuhr, the author of this prayer, was a Christian minister, and he reminded himself of the way Christ acted toward this world. Christ came to provide a way back to God through obedience to God's will. He didn't seek to control or overpower people's will—people have freedom to choose. And Christ understood that men may choose evil.

So Niebuhr reminded himself in prayer that, whereas *he*

might choose obedience to God's will for his life, *others* may choose their own will. And that has often meant war, crime, poverty, injustice, and suffering for the innocent. We will never know serenity or peace of mind until we take this world as is, not as we would have it. This was Niebuhr's way of saying "stuff happens!"

"Trusting that you will make all things right if I surrender to your will." This petition is the very expression of Step Three, where we make a decision to turn our will and our lives over to the care of God as we understand God. We would never make the Step Three decision if we did not trust that our Higher Power could "make all things right." This particular petition is a wonderful Step Three declaration worthy of being prayed daily.

The final petition is a poignant affirmation of faith and hope, *"That I may be reasonably happy in this life, and supremely happy with you forever in the next."* Included with this affirmation is the realistic understanding that in this life "reasonably happy" is all we can really expect. But the hope of eternal life and happiness is an enduring source of comfort in the midst of daily, temporal hardships.

❦ ❦ ❦

Serenity Prayer

God, grant me
The serenity to accept the things I cannot change;
The courage to change the things I can; and
The wisdom to know the difference.
Living one day at a time;
Enjoying one moment at a time;
Accepting hardship as the pathway to peace;
Taking, as you did, this sinful world as it is,
not as I would have it;
Trusting that you will make all things right
if I surrender to your will;
That I may be reasonably happy in this life,
and supremely happy with you forever in the next.

Changes

Today I pray that I may understand there are some
    things I cannot change:
I cannot change the weather.
I cannot change the tick of the clock.
I cannot change the past.
I cannot change other people against their will.
I cannot change what is right and wrong.
I cannot change the fact that a relationship ended.
I can stop worrying over that which I cannot change and
    enjoy living more!
I can place those things into the hands of the _One who is_
    bigger than I. Save energy. Let go. Instead of trying to
    change someone else:

I can change my attitude.
I can change my list of priorities.
I can change my bad habits into good ones.
I can move from the place of brokenness into wholeness,
    into the beautiful person God created me to become.

The Gifts I Ask

These are the gifts I ask of thee, Spirit serene:
    Strength for the daily task,
    Courage to face the road,
    Good cheer to help me
    Bear the traveler's load;
    And for the hours that come between,
    An inward joy in all things heard and seen.

The Acceptance Prayer

God grant me the serenity to accept my addiction
gracefully and humbly. Grant me also the ability to
absorb the teachings of the program, which by its past
experience is trying to help me. Teach me to be grateful
for the help I receive.

Guide me, Higher Power, in the path of tolerance
and understanding of my fellow members and fellow
humans, guide me away from the path of criticism,
intolerance, jealousy, and envy of my friends. Let me
not prejudge; let me not become a moralist; keep my
tongue and thoughts from malicious idle gossip.

Help me to grow in stature spiritually, mentally,
and morally. Grant me that greatest of all rewards,
that of being able to help my fellow sufferers in their

search out of the addiction that has encompassed them.

Above all, help me to be less critical and impatient with myself.

God, Help Me Live Today

God, more than anything else in this world, I just don't
  want to be sick any more.
God, grant me the serenity to accept the things I cannot
  change (people, places, and things),
The courage to change the things I can (my attitudes),
And the common sense to know the difference.
God, help me, please, stay clean and sober this day, even
  if it's in spite of myself. Help me Lord, stay sensitive
  to my own needs and the things that are good for me,
  the needs of others and the things that are good for
  them.
And if you please, Lord, free me enough of the bondage
  of self that I may be of some useful value as a human
  being, whether I understand or not,
That I may carry my own keys, maintain my own
  integrity, and live this day at peace with you, at
  peace with myself, and at peace with the world I
  live in, just for today.
God help me in this day demonstrate that:
  It is good for me to love and to be loved.
  It is good for me to understand and to be understood.
  It is good for me to give and to receive.
  It is good for me to comfort and to allow myself to be
  comforted.
And it is obviously far better for me to be useful as a
  human being, than it is to be selfish.
God, help me please put one foot in front of the other,

keep moving forward, and do the best I can with
what I have to work with today,
Accepting the results of whatever that may or may not be.

Today's Thought

Lord,
I am but one, but I am one;
I can't do everything,
But I can do *something;*
What I can do, I ought to do;
What I ought to do, with your help,
I will do.

This I Believe

God, tomorrow is yet to be,
But should you grant me another day,
The hope, courage, and strength
Through the working of the Twelve Steps and Serenity
    Prayer,
I shall be sufficiently provided for to meet my every need.
This I believe.

14

Prayers *for* the Recovery Community

Dear Higher Power,
I am grateful that I am part of
the fellowship, one among many,
but I am one.

🍎 "HELLO?"

"Is Dan there?" the woman asked.

"Yeah, but he's getting ready."

"For what?"

"He's getting a chip tonight. It's his birthday!"

"Like hell it's his birthday! This is his mother," she barked. "Put him on the phone."

"Mom, how are you?" Dan timidly asked.

"What does he mean that it's your birthday? Your birthday is three months away." Her demanding tone set Dan's jaw and tempted him to hang up.

"You wouldn't understand, Mom."

"What sort of foolishness are you up to? Why can't you be normal? You're an embarrassment to me. You know that don't you?"

Silence…

"Well? Answer me!"

"Bye, Mom."

"What did your mom want, Dan?"

"She wanted…I don't know, man. I don't know what she wanted. But *I want* to see my family. Let's go to the meeting."

THOSE OF US IN A TWELVE-STEP PROGRAM ARE A PART of a large family, the recovery community. Whatever our addiction, compulsion, obsession, or drug of choice, we all have one thing in common. We struggle with the control disease. We were controlled as children. Then the pain of being violated (whatever form) and overpowered by another (something God has chosen never to do) controls us. So we respond through control. We control the pain of loss through food. We control the feeling of being belittled through controlling others with bravado and arrogance. We control the pain of self-hatred that says "You were a damn mistake!" through alcohol or drugs. We control the agony of…through….

Then the drug of choice has its own curse, and we reap it. A part of that curse is guilt, which reinforces our pain and feelings of worthlessness. So we cling tighter to people if we are codependents; we reach out more to drugs if we are addicts; we nurse a bottle if we're alcoholic. We ease our pain through sex if we are bent that way; we cherish our sickness and lick up the attention of doctors and pharmacists if we so choose; we bury our pain under mounds and hours of work.

And maybe when nothing will quiet the pain, we quit.

There are two ways of quitting. Some quitters never return—they rest cold. The other type of quitters surrender—they trust another, their Higher Power. The recovery community trusts God, a Power greater.

In the recovery community we find safety, anonymity, acceptance, tolerance, fellowship, and, greatest of all, we find understanding. When we go to a meeting, we hear our story in the stories of others. They know how we feel because they live it, too. Has anyone ever expressed feelings of worthlessness, self-hatred, or fear without everyone feeling the pain? No. Not in the recovery community.

From the meetings to the roundups, the workshops, the activities, the spiritual meetings, and the national conferences—we come together. From the fellowship of friends to the trust of confidants and the guidance of sponsors—we share our lives one with another. Together we work principles, steps that heal, spiritual principles that restore our worth, our self-esteem, our right to draw breath and exist.

We fellowship around our common desire—no—our common need, the need for recovery and sanity. And we find that recovery and sanity as we transfer our need to control to our Higher Power—as we seek God's will. We find that God alone has the wisdom, love, and power to direct our lives.

Because of our connection to the recovery community, we learn to pray for and with our family of fellow travelers on the road to recovery. A prayer for the recovery community might say, "Higher Power, I thank you for such an understanding community. Bless them, and help me contribute to the common good."

Meeting Prayer No. 1

Our Father, we come to you as a friend.

You have said that, where two or three are gathered in your name, there you will be in the midst. We believe you are with us now.

We believe this is something you would have us do, and that it has your blessing.

We believe that you want us to be real partners with you in this business of living, accepting our full responsibility and certain that the rewards will be freedom, growth, and happiness.

For this, we are grateful.

We ask you, at all times, to guide us.

Help us daily to come closer to you, and grant us new ways of living our gratitude.

Meeting Prayer No. 2

Higher Power of our fellowship,

We ask your blessings on this meeting. Please bless the spirit and the purpose of this group.

Give us strength to follow this program according to your will and in all humility.

Forgive us for yesterday, and grant us courage for today and hope for tomorrow.

Meeting Prayer No. 3

God bless this meeting and the members gathered here.

Help us to make this group a haven of strength and comfort, giving to all who seek help here the beauty and friendliness of home, which shall be as a shield against temptation of all kinds and against loneliness and despair.

Bless those who are going forth from this house to fight the gallant fight, to know suffering; and bless those who come here to rest, those who must readjust themselves to face life once more.

The Fellowship Prayer

Dear Higher Power, I am grateful that:
I am part of the fellowship, one among many, but I am
   one.

I need to work the steps for the development of the buried life within me.

Our program may be human in its organization, but it is divine in its purpose. The purpose is to continue my spiritual awakening.

Participating in the privileges of the movement, I shall share in the responsibilities, taking it upon myself to carry my fair share of the load, not grudgingly, but joyfully.

To the extent that I fail in my responsibilities, the program fails. To the extent that I succeed, the program succeeds.

I shall not wait to be drafted for service to my fellow members. I shall volunteer.

I shall be loyal in my attendance, generous in my giving, kind in my criticism, creative in my suggestions, loving in my attitudes.

I shall give to the program my interest, my enthusiasm, my devotion, most of all...myself.

Am I Willing?

Dear Higher Power, help me:

To forget what I have done for other people, and to remember what other people have done for me.

To ignore what the world owes me, and to think what I owe the world.

To put my rights in the background, and my duties in the middle distance, and my chances to do a little more than my duty in the foreground.

To see that my fellow members are just as real as I am, and to try to look behind their faces to their hearts, as hungry for joy as mine is.

To own that probably the only good reason for my
existence is not what I can get out of life but what
I can give to life.
To close my book of complaints against the management
of the universe and look for a place where I can sow
a few seeds of happiness—am I willing to do these
things even for a day?
Then I have a good chance of staying with the program.

Kindness and Service

O Lord, help me always to remember thankfully the
work of those who helped me when I needed help.
Reward them for their kindness and service,
and grant that I may have the will, the time, and the
opportunity to do the same for others.

The Tolerance Prayer

Lord, give me tolerance toward those whose thoughts
and ways, in the program and life, conflict with mine, for
though I would, I cannot always know what constitutes
the Absolute Truth. The other person may be right, while
I may be all wrong, yet unaware.

Lord, make my motives right, for only this can ease
my conscience when I sometimes err.

Lord, give me tolerance, for who am I to stand in
judgment on another person's mistakes. No one knows
better than my inward self how many little blunders I
have and can make.

Life is full of stones that somehow trip us and
meaning not, we stumble now and then.

Lord, give me tolerance, for only you are rightly fit to judge my fellow travelers.

The Way

Dear Lord, today I pray:
The way is long
Let us go together.
The way is difficult
Let us help each other.
The way is joyful
Let us share it.
The way is ours alone
Let us go in love.
The way grows before us
Let us begin.

The Victims of Addiction

O blessed Lord, you ministered to all who came to you.
Look with compassion upon all who through addiction have lost their health and freedom. Restore to them the assurance of your unfailing mercy; remove from them the fears that beset them; strengthen them in the work of their recovery; and to those who care for them, give patient understanding and persevering love.

Fellow Travelers

Higher Power, who fills our whole life, and whose presence we find wherever we go, preserve us who travel the road of recovery, surround us with your loving care, protect us from every danger, and bring us in safety to our journey's end.

For Those Who Have Relapsed

O God of all mercies and comfort, who helps us in time of need, we humbly ask you to behold, visit, and relieve those who have relapsed, for whom our prayers are desired. Look upon them with the eyes of your mercy; comfort them with a sense of your goodness; preserve them from the temptations of their addiction; and give them patience under their affliction. In your time, restore them to the program and physical, mental, and spiritual health. And help them, we pray, to listen, believe, and do your will.

An Irish Blessing

May the road rise to meet you,
May the wind be always at your back.
May the sun shine warm on your face,
The rain fall softly on your fields,
And until we meet again,
May God hold you in the palm of his hand.

My Prayer for You

I thought of you so much today
I went to God in prayer,

To ask him to watch over you
And show you that we care.

My prayer for you was not for rewards
That you could touch or feel,
But true rewards for happiness
That are so very real.

Like love and understanding
In all the things you do,
And guidance when you need it most
To see your troubles through.

I asked him for good health for you
So your future could be bright,
And faith to accept life's challenges
And the courage to do what's right.

I gave thanks to him for granting my prayer
To bring you peace and love.
May you feel the warmth in your life
With God's blessings from above.

Tolerance Prayer

Higher Power, help me to know the most lovable
quality I can possess is tolerance. It is the vision that
enables me to see things from another's viewpoint. It is
the generosity that concedes to others the right to their
own opinions and their own peculiarities. It is the bigness
that enables me to let people be happy in their own way
instead of my way.

I Cannot Pray

I cannot pray the Lord's Prayer and even once say "I."
I cannot pray the Lord's Prayer and even once say "my."
Nor can I pray the Lord's Prayer and not pray for
    another,
And when I ask for daily bread, I must include my
    brother.
For others are included in each and every plea,
From the beginning to the end of it, it does not once
    say "me."

Living the Way We Pray

I knelt to pray when day was done
And prayed: "O Lord, bless everyone,
And lift from each heart the pain,
And let the sick be well again."

And then the next day when I did awake,
I carelessly went on my way.
The whole day long I did not try
To wipe a tear from any eye.

I did not try to share the load
Of any brother on the road.
I did not even go to see
The sick man just next door to me.

Yet once again when day was done
I prayed: "O Lord, bless everyone."
But as I prayed, to my ear
There came a voice that whispered clear:

"Pause, hypocrite, before you pray:
Whom have you tried to bless today?
God's sweetest blessings always go
By hands that serve him here below."

Conclusion

THERE IS NOTHING WRONG WITH PRAYING PRAYERS that are already written. But there is something special about praying prayers that are our very own—prayers forged in the fires of our own pain, suffering, and struggle; prayers recast through our own experience, strength, and hope; and prayers never before spoken—just between us and our Higher Power.

The prayers in this guide are more than prayers to say what we cannot seem to express. They are intended as examples, too. Examples to aid us in the creation of our own prayers. We can make prayer personal. We can write, speak, express, cry, sing, moan, laugh, act out, or scream our own prayers to God. It doesn't matter how. But it does matter.